My Visit to the Hospital

Paul Humphrey

Photography by Chris Fairclough

W
FRANKLIN WATTS
LONDON • SYDNEY

First published in 2007 by
Franklin Watts
338 Euston Road
London NW1 3BH

Franklin Watts Australia
Level 17/207 Kent Street
Sydney NSW 2000

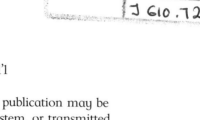

ISBN: 978 0 7496 7456 4 (hbk)
ISBN: 978 0 7496 7468 7 (pbk)

Dewey classification number: 362.1'1

A CIP catalogue record for this book is available from the British Library.

Planning and production by Discovery Books Limited
Editors: Rachel Tisdale and James Nixon
Designer: Ian Winton
Photography: Chris Fairclough
Series advisors: Diana Bentley MA and Dee Reid MA,
Fellows of Oxford Brookes University

The author, packager and publisher would like to thank the following
people for their participation in this book: Georgia, Molly and Rebecca
Haywood, Amanda Moore and the staff at Kidderminster Hospital.

All photographs by Chris Fairclough.

Printed in China

Franklin Watts is a division of Hachette Children's Books, an Hachette Livre UK company.

Contents

A broken ankle

Georgia fell off her bike and broke her ankle.

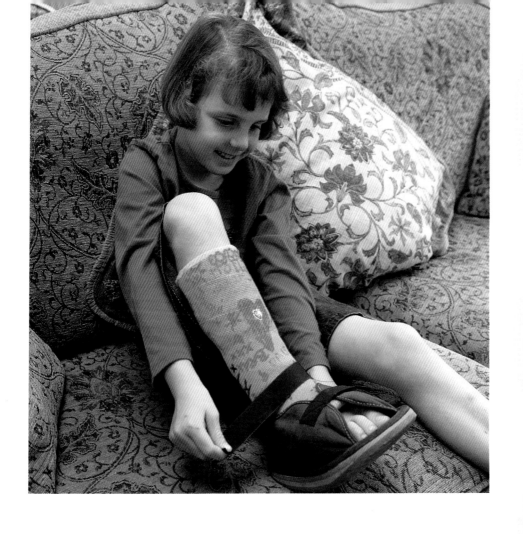

She has been wearing
a plaster cast.

Going to hospital

Now Georgia's ankle is better.

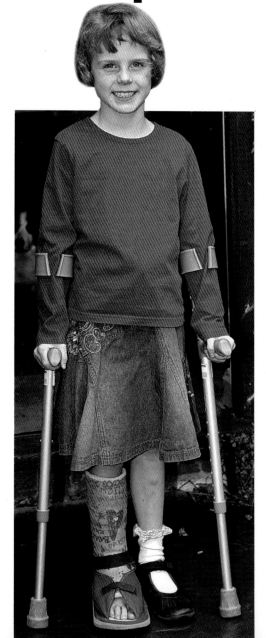

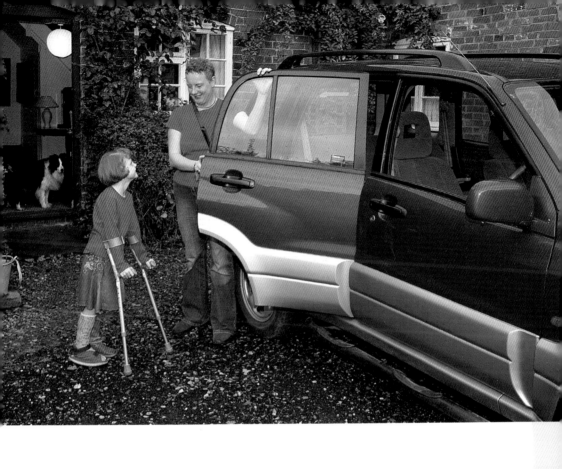

She is going to
hospital to have the
plaster cast taken off.

At the hospital

Georgia and her mum arrive at the hospital.

9

Waiting area

Georgia tells the receptionist her name.

Please take a seat.

Georgia and Mum sit in the waiting area.

The doctor

Georgia waits to see the doctor.

The doctor tells her she must have an x-ray.

It won't hurt.

X-ray

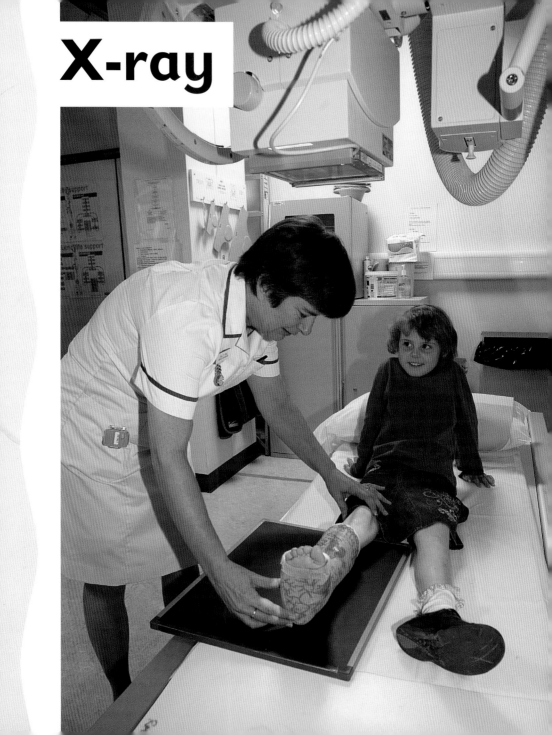

A machine takes
an x-ray picture.

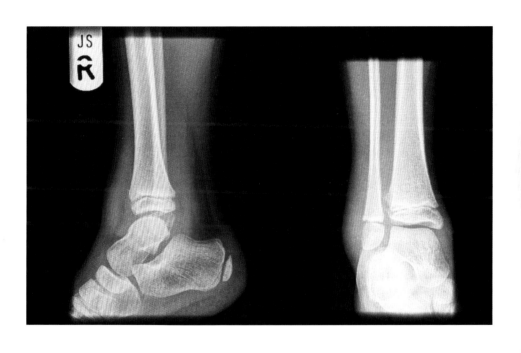

The bone in Georgia's
ankle has mended.

Cutting the plaster cast

Then Georgia goes to a different room.

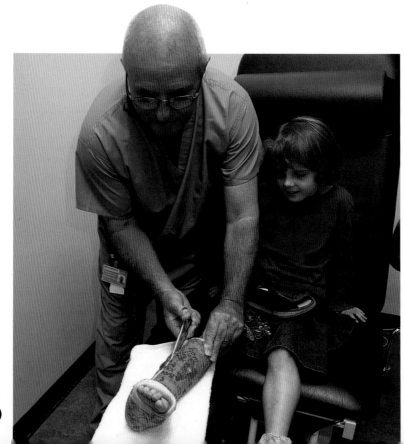

16

A nurse cuts off the plaster cast.

Standing up

The nurse looks at Georgia's ankle.

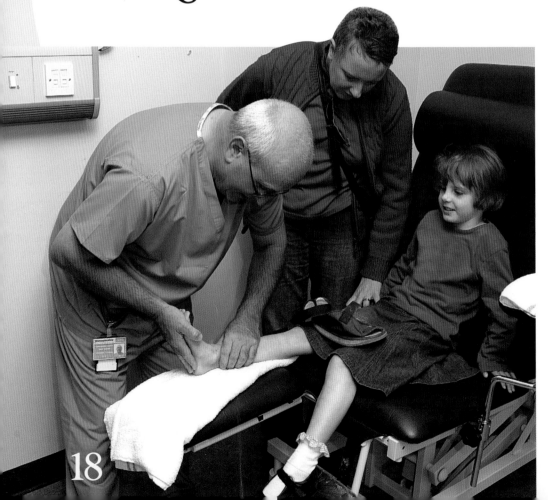

He asks her to stand up.

How does that feel?

Great!

Going home

Georgia is happy that her plaster cast is off.

It is time to go home.

Riding a bike!

A few weeks later, Georgia's leg is stronger.

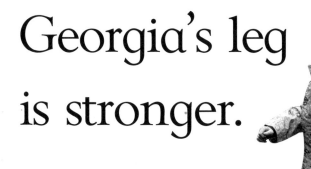

She can
ride her
bike again!

Word bank

Look back for these words and pictures.

Ankle

Doctor

Hospital

Nurse

Plaster cast

Receptionist

Waiting area

X-ray

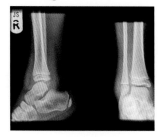

X-ray machine